Lerner SPORTS

ALL-STAR SMACKDOWN

JUSTIN JEFFERSON VS. RANDY MOSS

WHO WOULD WIN?

JIM GIGLIOTTI

Lerner Publications ◆ Minneapolis

Lerner Publications Company
An imprint of Lerner Publishing Group, Inc.
241 First Avenue North
Minneapolis, MN 55401 USA

For reading levels and more information, look up this title at www.lernerbooks.com.

Main body text set in Aptifer Sans LT Pro.
Typeface provided by Linotype AG.

Library of Congress Cataloging-in-Publication Data

Names: Gigliotti, Jim, author.
Title: Justin Jefferson vs. Randy Moss : who would win? / Jim Gigliotti.
Description: Minneapolis, MN : Lerner Publications, [2025] | Series:
All-star smackdown | Includes bibliographical references and index. | Audience: Ages 7–11 | Audience: Grades 2–3 | Summary: "Wide receivers Randy Moss and Justin Jefferson are human highlight reels. Their speed, athleticism, and big personalities make them NFL legends. But which superstar is better? Explore their careers and make your own decision"— Provided by publisher.
Identifiers: LCCN 2023035529 (print) | LCCN 2023035530 (ebook) | ISBN 9798765625897 (library binding) | ISBN 9798765628133 (paperback) | ISBN 9798765632161 (epub)
Subjects: LCSH: Jefferson, Justin, 1999—Juvenile literature. | Moss, Randy,—Juvenile literature. | Football players—United States—Biography—Juvenile literature. | Wide receivers (Football)—United States—Biography—Juvenile literature.
Classification: LCC GV939.J44 G54 2025 (print) | LCC GV939.J44 (ebook) | DDC 796.332092 [B]—dc23/eng/20230805

LC record available at https://lccn.loc.gov/2023035529
LC ebook record available at https://lccn.loc.gov/2023035530

Manufactured in the United States of America
1 – CG – 7/15/24

TABLE OF CONTENTS

Randy Moss

INTRODUCTION

TWO FOOTBALL STARS

Minnesota Vikings fans are lucky. For many years, Randy Moss starred for the team. He was one of the best wide receivers in the National Football League (NFL). Moss left the Vikings after the 2004 season. But in 2020, the team added Justin Jefferson, another pass-catching superstar.

Fast Facts

- Randy Moss set an NFL record with 23 touchdown catches in 2007.
- Moss had 156 touchdown catches, the second most ever.
- Justin Jefferson was the NFL Offensive Player of the Year in 2022.
- Jefferson led the NFL in both catches and receiving yards in 2022.

Moss and Jefferson are both known for their amazing skill. Moss became famous for incredible leaping catches when he entered the NFL in 1998. In the first quarter of his first game, Moss showed what he could do. He jumped for a long pass at the same time a Tampa Bay Buccaneers player jumped. Moss tipped the pass to himself. He caught it and stepped into the end zone for a touchdown!

Justin Jefferson

Vikings fans never thought they'd see another receiver dominate opponents the way that Moss did. Then Justin Jefferson joined the team.

In 2022, he made an all-time great catch. It was fourth down and 18 yards to go against the Buffalo Bills. The game was on the line. Jefferson leaped high for a pass. With one hand, he pulled it out of the defender's hands. Fans were amazed at the awesome play!

Minnesota fans have enjoyed watching both superstars. But which player is better? That's up to you to decide. Let the smackdown begin!

Randy Moss played for the Vikings from 1998 to 2004.

This leaping catch by Jefferson in 2022 helped make him famous around the NFL.

CHAPTER 1

Moss's photo hangs in the hallway of his high school in West Virginia.

THE ROAD TO THE NFL

Randy Moss grew up as a big star in a small town. He was born on February 13, 1977, in Rand, West Virginia. Rand has a population of fewer than 2,000 people. In high school, Moss was a baseball, basketball, and track-and-field star. But his best sport was football. His team won two state championships. College coaches were impressed with how good Moss already was as a teenager.

Moss accepted an offer to play college football at the University of Notre Dame. But he made a mistake and got into a high school fight. As a result of the fight, Notre Dame took back their offer. Moss attended Florida State University instead.

Moss spent one season at Florida State. But he made another mistake by using an illegal drug. Florida State's coach cut him from the team. In 1997, Moss started at Marshall University in West Virginia.

In 1997, his hard work and talent earned him the Biletnikoff Award for college football's best receiver. The next year, the Vikings took him with the 21st overall pick of the NFL Draft. Moss promised the team's head coach, Dennis Green, that he would not disappoint him.

In 1997, Moss set a US college record with 26 touchdown catches.

Moss caught 69 passes in 1998, including this catch against the Tennessee Oilers.

Moss kept his promise to Coach Green and avoided mistakes off the field. On the field, he was terrific. In his first game, he scored two touchdowns. That season, he caught 17 touchdown passes, an NFL rookie record.

Moss was just getting started. He went on to play 14 seasons in the NFL and made the Pro Bowl six times. He finished his career with 156 touchdown catches, the second most in league history.

This touchdown catch in a 2003 game helped Moss lead the NFL with 17.

Justin Jefferson was born on June 16, 1999. He grew up in Destrehan, Louisiana. He was a good player in high school, but he didn't impress college coaches the way Moss did.

High school players are rated from one to five stars. Players with more stars are expected to be better in college. Moss was a five-star player. Jefferson was only a three-star player.

Jefferson enrolled in nearby Louisiana State University (LSU) in 2017. He didn't catch any passes his first year in college. But by his third year, he led the nation in catches and LSU won the national championship.

Jefferson **(bottom)** *had 54 catches in 2018, his second season with LSU.*

Jefferson had 18 touchdown catches for LSU in 2019.

Jefferson runs with the ball during the 2022 Pro Bowl.

The Vikings chose Jefferson with the 22nd overall pick of the 2020 NFL Draft. He made an immediate impact his rookie season. By the third game, he was a starter. He racked up 175 receiving yards in that game! Jefferson went on to break Moss's record for catches by a Vikings rookie. Jefferson had more receiving yards than any other rookie since 1960. He was one of only two NFL rookies to make the Pro Bowl.

CONSIDER THIS

Moss set an NFL rookie record when he caught 17 touchdown passes in 1998. Jefferson had only seven touchdowns in his rookie year. That season, Jefferson caught 88 passes for 1,400 yards. Moss caught 69 passes for 1,313 yards in his first season.

Jefferson's speed helps him gain a lot of yards after making a catch.

CHAPTER 2

Moss heads for the end zone against the Dallas Cowboys on Thanksgiving in 1998.

GREATEST MOMENTS

Football fans in Minnesota knew about Randy Moss from the start of his career. NFL fans everywhere learned his name on Thanksgiving of his rookie season. That day, Moss caught only three passes against the Cowboys. But they were all jaw-dropping catches.

The first came on the fourth play of the game. It was a 51-yard touchdown. The second came late in the first quarter when Moss caught a 56-yard touchdown. The third catch was another 56-yard touchdown in the third quarter. Moss had three catches for 163 yards and three scores. Moss was too fast and talented for the Cowboys defense. The Vikings won, 46–36. Moss was on his way to becoming one of the all-time greats.

Moss played for the Vikings through 2004. Then he played for several teams before retiring in 2010. In 2012, he came back for one more year of football, this time with the San Francisco 49ers. Everywhere he went, it was the same story. He had a lot of catches, yards, and touchdowns. After the 2012 season, he retired for good. In 2018, Moss joined the Pro Football Hall of Fame.

Moss spent 2005 and 2006 with the Oakland Raiders.

Jefferson escapes a Tennessee Titans defender to complete a 71-yard touchdown.

Jefferson didn't start the first two games of his rookie season. By Week 3, he was in the starting lineup for the first time. He had 175 receiving yards that day against the Tennessee Titans. One of his seven catches was a 71-yard touchdown. The next week, he had 103 yards on just four catches in a win over the Houston Texans. By the season's end, he had seven 100-yard games. That broke Randy Moss's previous team record of four.

CONSIDER THIS

Justin Jefferson had at least 100 receiving yards in a game 24 times in his first three years in the NFL. That was more than any other NFL player achieved during their first three years. Randy Moss shared the record of 19 100-yard games before Jefferson beat it.

One of Jefferson's greatest moments was his fourth-down catch against the Bills in 2022. Not only did he take the ball away from a defender, he also kept it from hitting the ground.

Jefferson is not as fast as some other receivers, including Moss. But Jefferson has great agility. And he knows how to position himself on the field. More often than not, he beats defenders to the ball.

Jefferson pulls the ball out of a Bills defender's hands to make this catch.

CHAPTER 3

Moss set records everywhere he played.

RECORD-SETTING SEASONS

For a receiver in the NFL, gaining 1,000 yards catching passes is a great year. Randy Moss played 14 seasons in the league. He had more than 1,000 receiving yards in seven of them. In 2003, he caught 111 passes for a whopping 1,632 yards. The receiving yards set a Vikings team record. In his first year with the New England Patriots in 2007, Moss caught 98 passes for 1,493 yards. That set a Patriots team record for yards.

Scoring touchdowns, though, is what Moss did best. In 2007, he caught an incredible 23 touchdown passes during the regular season. That was more than any other NFL player had ever caught. More importantly, Moss helped the Patriots win all 16 of their games.

Winning is a common theme with both Moss and Jefferson. During Moss's NFL career, his teams made the playoffs seven times. In college, Jefferson helped LSU win the national championship. In 2022, he helped the Vikings win 13 games.

Moss (right) celebrates one of his 23 touchdown catches with his Patriots teammates.

In 2021, Jefferson had 1,616 receiving yards. That was only 16 yards short of the Vikings record that Moss set in 2003. But in 2022, Jefferson was even better. He caught 128 passes for 1,809 yards. He led the NFL in catches and yards and set new Vikings season records.

CONSIDER THIS

Justin Jefferson had 4,825 receiving yards in his first three NFL seasons. That was more than any other player in NFL history. Randy Moss racked up 4,163 yards over his first three years.

In 2022, Jefferson (left) *and Adam Thielen* (right) *celebrated a Thanksgiving win with turkey legs.*

Jefferson's total of 1,809 receiving yards in 2022 was the sixth highest in NFL history.

CHAPTER 4

Moss at the Pro Football Hall of Fame in 2018

AND THE WINNER IS

Almost from the moment that Justin Jefferson first pulled on his purple Vikings jersey, Minnesota fans asked if he could become the next Randy Moss. After watching Jefferson play, fans around the NFL are wondering if he might be even better. So who wins this wide receiver smackdown?

Moss was the faster runner. But Jefferson may have the best body control of any receiver in the NFL. He can keep his hands on the ball even while leaping or diving. Moss was a touchdown machine. Jefferson is piling up yards faster than any other player in league history.

Moss's name is all over the Vikings record book. But it seems like almost every time Jefferson takes the field, he sets another record of his own.

In a 2022 game against the Detroit Lions, Jefferson had 223 receiving yards to set a new Vikings record. He caught 10 or more passes in six of Minnesota's 16 games that season. The team won five of those games. At season's end, he won the NFL Offensive Player of the Year award.

Jefferson caught 324 passes in his first three seasons with the Vikings.

Moss had a great career that lasted 14 seasons. But Jefferson's early career numbers are better than Moss's. There is a good chance that he will break many of Moss's records if he stays healthy.

Our smackdown winner is Jefferson! Moss had a long career and broke many records. But what Jefferson has done in a short time in the NFL is too great to ignore. There's no wrong answer. Who do you think wins this smackdown? Consider their stories and make your choice!

Moss poses with Vikings kicker Gary Anderson before the 1999 Pro Bowl in Hawaii.

Jefferson has said he wants to be the greatest wide receiver in NFL history.

SMACKDOWN BREAKDOWN

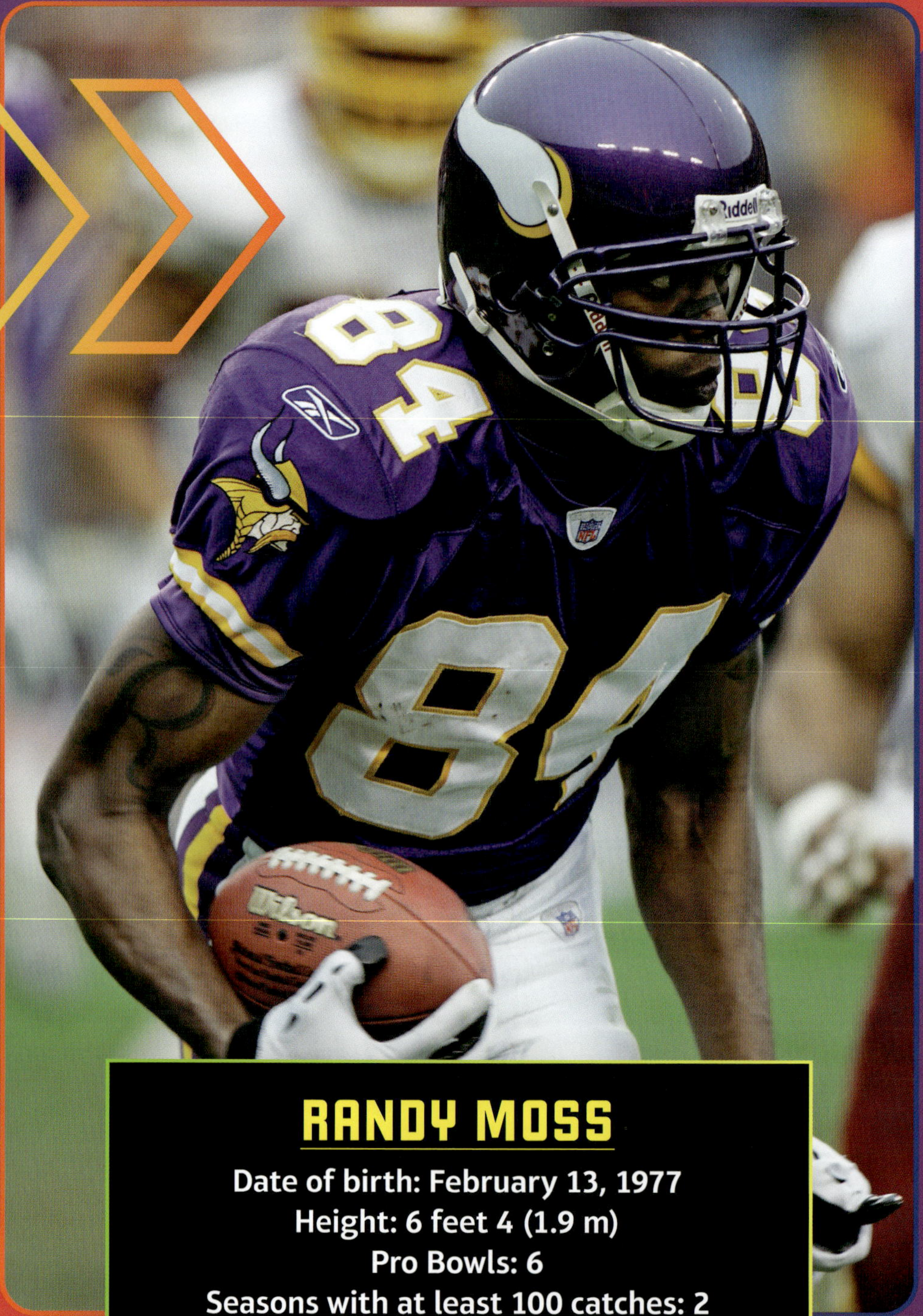

RANDY MOSS

Date of birth: February 13, 1977
Height: 6 feet 4 (1.9 m)
Pro Bowls: 6
Seasons with at least 100 catches: 2
Seasons with at least 1,000 receiving yards: 10

Stats are accurate through the 2023 NFL season.

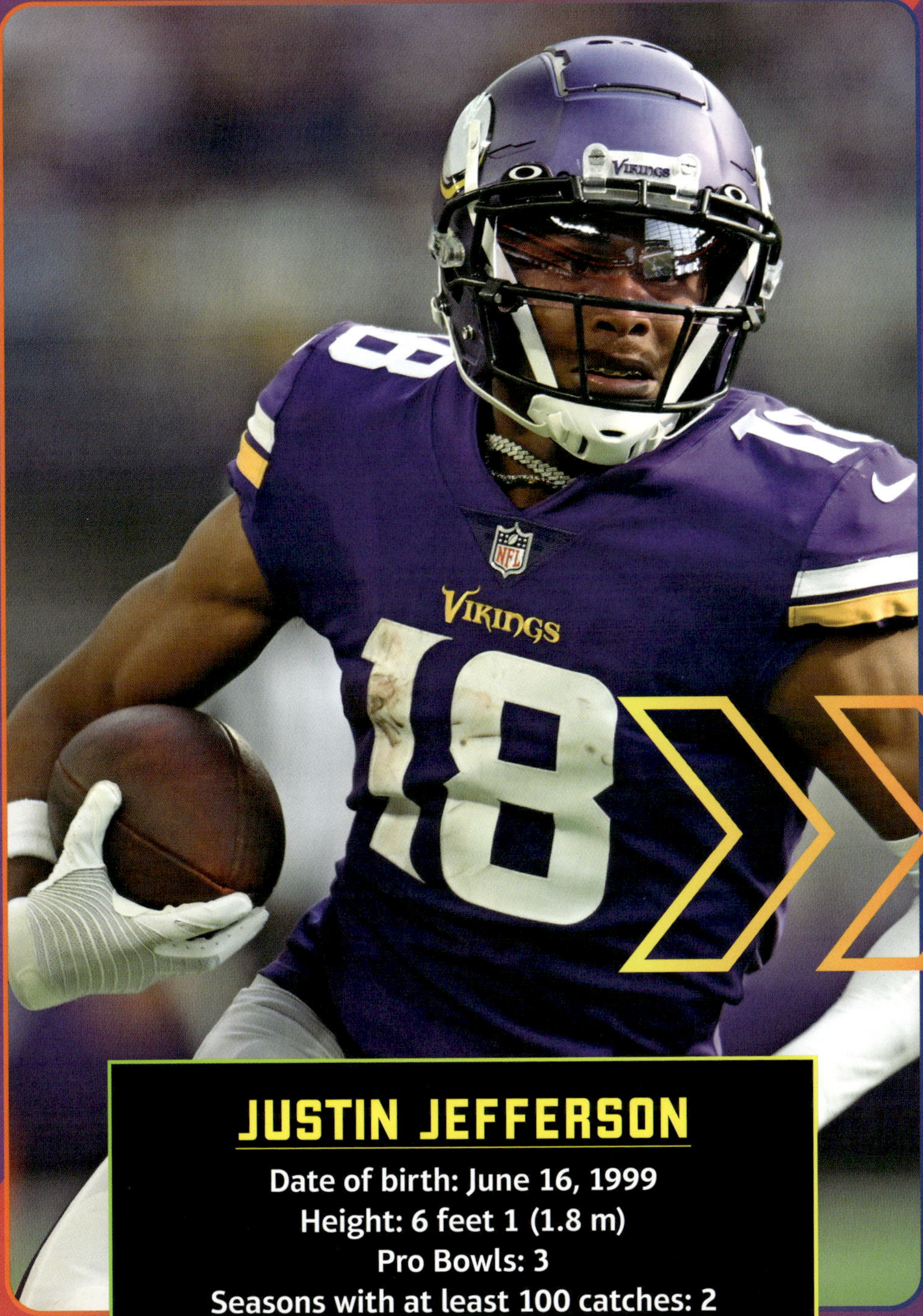

JUSTIN JEFFERSON

Date of birth: June 16, 1999
Height: 6 feet 1 (1.8 m)
Pro Bowls: 3
Seasons with at least 100 catches: 2
Seasons with at least 1,000 receiving yards: 4

GLOSSARY

agility: the ability to move easily and quickly

draft: when teams take turns choosing new players

end zone: the area at each end of a football field where players score touchdowns

playoffs: a series of games played to decide a champion

Pro Bowl: the NFL's all-star game

regular season: when all of the teams in a league play one another to determine playoff teams

rookie: a first-year player

starter: a player in the lineup at the beginning of a game

wide receiver: a football player whose main job is to catch passes

LEARN MORE

Anderson, Josh. *Inside the Minnesota Vikings.* Minneapolis: Lerner Publications, 2024.

Coleman, Ted. *Minnesota Vikings All-Time Greats.* Mendota Heights, MN: North Star Editions, 2021.

LSU Football
https://lsusports.net/sports/fb/

Mitchell, Bo. *Justin Jefferson.* Mendota Heights, MN: North Star Editions, 2023.

Smith, Elliott. *Meet Justin Jefferson.* Minneapolis: Lerner Publications, 2024.

Sports Illustrated Kids: Football
https://www.sikids.com/football

INDEX

PHOTO ACKNOWLEDGMENTS

Focus on Football, p. 4; Focus on Football, p. 5; Carlos Gonzalez/ZUMA Press/Newscom, p. 6; Lauren Bacho via AP, p. 7; AP Photo/Jeff Gentner, p. 8; RVR Photos-USA TODAY Sports, p. 9; AP Photo/Scott Boehm, p. 10; Joe Ledford/KRT/Newscom, p. 11; AP Photo/Matthew Hinton, p. 12; AP Photo/Rick Scuteri, p. 13; AP Photo/Rick Scuteri, p. 14; Focus on Football, p. 15; AP Photo/Tim Sharp, p. 16; Focus on Football, p. 17; Carlos Gonzalez/Star Tribune via AP, p. 18; AP Photo/ Jeffrey T. Barnes, p. 19; Focus on Football, p. 20; AP Photo/Winslow Townson, p. 21; Matt Krohn-USA TODAY Sports, p. 22; AP Photo/Ryan Kang, p. 23; Rich Graessle/Icon Sportswire/Newscom, p. 24; Focus on Football, p. 25; Paul Spinelli via AP, 26; Jeffrey Becker-USA TODAY Sports, p. 27; Focus on Football, p. 28; Jeffrey Becker-USA TODAY Sports, p. 29.

Cover: Jeffrey Becker-USA TODAY Sports (Justin Jefferson James Lang-USA TODAY Sports (Randy Moss).